No Dice

Published by 404 Ink Limited
www.404Ink.com
@404Ink

Please note: Some references include URLs which may change or be unavailable after publication of this book. All references within endnotes were accessible and accurate as of September 2022 but may experience link rot from there on in.

Editing: Laura Jones
Typesetting: Laura Jones
Cover design: Luke Bird
Co-founders and publishers of 404 Ink:
Heather McDaid & Laura Jones

Print ISBN: 978-1-912489-66-4
Ebook ISBN: 978-1-912489-67-1

Printed and bound in Great Britain by Clays Ltd, Elcograf S.p.A.

No Dice

Gambling and Risk in Modern Culture

Nathan Charles

Inklings

for my wonderful mother
my hilarious old man
my beautiful sister kate

love you all eternally

sorry for being such a little
shit in school

x

Contents

Introduction

Risk & Play

I am somebody that has never truly defined themselves as a gambling addict. I consider myself, rather, a person who has, at times, religiously gambled and taken risks. A person who has an addictive personality with an attraction to the uncertain. When somebody asks me whether I am a gambling addict, I say something along the lines of 'it's a complicated relationship' or, more often than not, 'I can only gamble what I can afford'. I am a person who likes to take risks.

When you begin looking into society's understanding of gambling and risk, with focus on the UK, it can be easy to get lost in the sheer amount of numbers, graphs, diagrams and statistics. Quantitative data forms the basis of shocking headlines and news articles buzzed to our phones. But what about the less obvious ways in which we gamble and take risks as consumers? How could you possibly link the *Pokémon* Trading Card Game with gambling? Compare Netflix to a night out in the West End? When does fictional gambling within video games go too far with their infamous loot boxes?

When I say 'gambling' you might picture a high-stakes Monaco casino, filled with dashing patrons in glamorous suits and frocks with sparkling jewellery to match. The reality is that gambling and the idea of risk is much closer to home then we realise, where fluffy dressing gowns and slippers are more the attire.

Throughout *No Dice* I am going to explore various forms of legal gambling embedded in popular culture, particularly within working class communities, that repeatedly avoid adequate legislative regulations, which I refer to as 'soft gambling' activities. For the context of this book, I define 'soft gambling' as an activity that is legal and either partly-regulated or not regulated at all, which requires an element of financial risk to participate in. A stake.

Research around the number of gamblers in the UK is skewed by prominent regulatory body the Gambling Commission and their definition of 'gambling': 'betting, gaming or participating in a lottery. That definition distinguishes between activities which need to be licensed and other activities which do not.'[1]

According to the NHS, developing a problematic

relationship with gambling can 'harm your health and relationships and leave you in serious debt'[2] amongst a whole host of other complications that are, of course, different with every individual case of addiction.

The NHS offers a questionnaire on their website to self-assess whether you may be, as they describe it, a 'problem gambler'.

Try this questionnaire:

- *Do you bet more than you can afford to lose?*
- *Do you need to gamble with larger amounts of money to get the same feeling?*
- *Have you tried to win back money you have lost (chasing losses)?*
- *Have you borrowed money or sold anything to get money to gamble?*
- *Have you wondered whether you have a problem with gambling?*
- *Has your gambling caused you any health problems, including feelings of stress or anxiety?*
- *Have other people criticised your betting or told you that you had a gambling problem (regardless of whether or not you thought it was true)?*
- *Has your gambling caused any financial problems for you or your household?*
- *Have you ever felt guilty about the way you gamble or what happens when you gamble?*

Score 0 for each time you answer "never"
Score 1 for each time you answer "sometimes"
Score 2 for each time you answer "most of the time"
Score 3 for each time you answer "almost always"

If your total score is 8 or higher, you may be a problem gambler.[3]

But what support is there for problem gamblers?

In 2002, under Tony Blair's Labour government, legislative measures were proposed to completely reform the gambling industry. Following a speech by then-Secretary of State for Culture, Media and Sport Tessa Jowell, a deal was struck with UK bookmakers and online betting companies to pave the way for problem gamblers to receive the help and care they needed. As a collective, the companies committed to giving 0.1 percent of their £14 billion revenues to charities such as BeGambleAware, an industry-leading organisation whose sole aim is to 'offer free, confidential help and support to anyone who's worried about their – or someone else's – gambling.'[4] Since then, the industry has 'increasingly failed to meet its commitments'[5] in its pledge. Investigative journalist Rob Davies revealed that '[betting] firms make at least 70 percent of their revenues from the biggest losers…'[6], indicating a clear financial incentive to keep vulnerable gamblers playing with them. Data released by BeGambleAware shows that 'some firms ensured their presence on the list [of donors] by giving just £1 or £5 a year.'[7]

Betting firms continue to show that financial gain comes above the well-being of their players, irrespective of vulnerability. Why would firms help treat the problem when they can simply *appear* to be helping and still reap the financial rewards of those with a problematic relationship with gambling, especially financially benefiting from those of less privileged backgrounds?

Russell Brand, comedian and addiction awareness activist, poses the question in his YouTube series: 'How can there ever be legislative change when the funding comes from the people benefitting from things saying the same?'[8], whether it be an extensive overhaul of rules and regulations or a mandatory tax on businesses that profit from gamblers.

* * *

> 'Now, when you think of working classness right, you lot wouldn't be wrong to think of the sort of gritty Channel 4 version of working class that tells you lot that my lot are opportunistic, taking what we can, doing as little as possible for it because that's all you know of it, that's all the tell, the papers, the news, your friends, your leaders tell you about us'.[9]

This quote is an extract from performance artist Scottee's show *Class*. I agree that the typical Channel 4 depictions of the working classes in their various documentaries over the years have been abhorrent but that is not the most interesting observation. The appeal Scottee mentions, of 'doing as little as possible' and pouncing on 'opportunities', isn't one I necessarily have a negative view on. Why wouldn't you, within the confines of the law, take an opportunity to earn money by 'doing as little as possible'? This makes me think about how the slog of a 12-hour shift on minimum wage compares to the chance of winning the same on a slot machine, or online roulette.

When I was 18, I had a job in a small café in Portsmouth Historic Dockyard on minimum wage. It wasn't the most glamorous job but certainly wasn't the most laborious. I was – and am still – grateful for that. I could go to work, earn my pay, and come home. I would commute on the bus every weekend without fail and situated next to the bus stop was a Ladbrokes betting shop, open 9am to 10pm every day. I would stand in its doorway and flag down my number 2 bus. At this point I'd never been in a traditional bookies before. I had placed bets online, sure, but never in a shop itself. I was intrigued.

After finishing work early one day, I popped in to place a bet on the Portsmouth FC match that I was going to that same evening. *One small bet,* I thought. I'd just earned £80.40 for my shift, what's ten pounds of that to put a bet on for? I could spend that on two beers so I'd just drink two fewer beers that evening. My bet came in and I earned more from the winnings than I did for my shift that day. The thought of staking ten pounds in the hope for a fruitful return was more appealing to me than the slog of another long shift.

According to a study by the University of Bristol, betting shops are 10 times more likely to be found in economically-deprived towns/cities than in affluent areas.[10] I've seen first-hand the appeal Scottee speaks of. You may notice prominent bookies on your travels to work or to the shops but where does soft gambling reside?

Before we dive into the messy world of soft gambling, I want you to set up a game to play. Throughout *No Dice* I'll ask you to answer a question about how gambling may have had a presence in your life, to reflect on an event that might have occurred. There is a box on the next page as an example.

If you're able to, **write in the box below the last risk you took**. If you're unable, I just want you to think about it for a moment. It could've just happened, or it could've happened years ago. Irrespective of time, I want you to think about the last time you did something that you consider to be a gamble.

Most readers of this book won't have any idea who I am. To you, I can't say thank you enough for taking a risk on this book. I hope that we get to the end of this together and you have a slightly better understanding of how the gambling mind functions. I hope you get to the end and feel as though you are in profit. That your investment in this book, both financially (if you have indeed parted with your hard-earned cash) and time spent reading, is worth it.

No Dice contains specific references to and depictions of forms of betting, gambling and risk which may be triggering to people with a gambling addiction, people who are currently in recovery, or define themselves (like me) as someone who has a tricky relationship with gambling. Support organisations and further information can be found on page 73.

Chapter 1
Loot Box Bonanza

Video games and betting are not often uttered in the same breath but in recent years there has been an increasingly worrying trend of video game developers implementing forms of unregulated in-game gambling that is readily accessible to anyone who buys their games, irrespective of age.

Developers Electronic Arts (EA) and Rockstar Games have long been accused of exploiting a legal gambling loophole by offering virtual 'loot boxes' to the players of their game, by players and betting charities. A loot box is generally defined as an electronic in-game item which can be redeemed to receive a variety of rewards. Players could purchase loot boxes, with real money, for the following reasons:

- **Increased Performance:** Loot boxes can give advantages to players purchasing them if they contain certain performance enhancing items otherwise unattainable.

- **Personalisation:** Opening boxes can provide in-game accessories, vehicles, aesthetic skins for a player's avatar or unlocking access to premium characters altogether, which are rare or are unable to be obtained through simply playing the game.

- **Obtaining Achievement:** Certain games only unlock and grant particular achievements and trophies when a purchase is made.

There is a clear appeal for gamers to buy into this pay-to-win model, whether the intention is to be the best in the game or simply have bragging rights over a friend for having an ultra-rare item. The Gambling Commission found that '23 percent of 11 to 16-year-olds had once opened an in-game online loot box'.[1] This is in part fuelled by the rise in video sharing and streaming sites such as Twitch, YouTube and Facebook Gaming and the content creators who use those sites to stream the opening of loot boxes across various games. Content creators such as W2S (1.1 million followers on Twitch at the time of writing) and Miniminter (1.8 million followers on Twitch) among others, have regularly produced videos of them opening loot boxes, each garnering millions of views and therefore the possibility of a substantial amount in potential advertising revenue or product placements brand deals that are placed on the video by the respective streaming platform.

The lure for viewers of these videos is typically that the higher the cost of the loot box, the higher the possibility of a rare reward, which can be a thrilling watch. Players will be willing to buy a loot box if the perceived value of the items is (potentially) higher than the cost. I place this game mechanic in our 'soft gambling' box, a tool in which players can, as Scottee says, 'do as little as possible'.

The most popular and profitable of loot boxes, amongst content creators, are within the *FIFA* collection of games. *FIFA 21* was 'ranked first among the top-selling video games in the United Kingdom in 2020 with sales of roughly 2.18 million'.[2] It is marketed by its creators, EA Sports, as:

> 'the largest sports video game franchise on the planet… letting you play with the biggest leagues, clubs, and players in world football… Whether you want to build your dream squad in FIFA Ultimate Team… the FIFA series lets you play The World's Game your way.'[3]

The FIFA Ultimate Team game mode mentioned continues to be the prime money-maker for EA Sports. EA earned record numbers in 2020 and one specific game-mode was responsible for a good chunk of their earnings, *Ultimate Team.*[4] Taking into account all sports games linked with EA Sports, including *FIFA* and *NFL*, EA generated a total of $1.49 billion through the Ultimate Team platform – a $120 million increase on 2019's revenue total of $1.37 billion.[5]

Loot boxes on the *FIFA Ultimate Team* platform come in the form of opening virtual trading card packs, not too dissimilar to the physical packs of *Match Attax* trading cards or *Panini* stickers you can buy in most convenience stores. In order to buy the electronic loot boxes, you have to first convert real cash into an in-game currency – 'FIFA Points' in this case. A 'Standard Pack' costs 150 FIFA points which in real terms costs the player £1, whereas the highest cost item is an 'Ultimate Pack' with an astronomical price-tag of 2,500 FIFA Points, equating to £16.66.

In previous years, there was no requirement for EA Sports to list what the odds of 'packing' a high-value item was, whereas if you were to buy a National Lottery scratch card, it is a legal requirement of the Gambling Commission that the odds of winning are printed clearly on the back of the card. The contract there is clear – if you were contemplating purchasing the scratch card you can see the exact odds of winning your money back in black and white. You could then make an informed decision as to whether you wanted to risk your money. The level of risk has not always been required to be clear for players opening loot boxes.

On 29th of June 2019, high-ranking employees of EA were summoned by the UK's Digital, Culture, Media and Sport Committee (DCMSC) to the Houses of Parliament, to present their argument and explain why they believed that loot boxes shouldn't be, legally, classified as a form of gambling in the UK and therefore more heavily regulated, like they currently are elsewhere in the world. Watching the proceedings unfold, it would have been easy to confuse the EA representatives with students who had rocked up to an exam, ill-prepared, with no revision under their belts, as they mumbled and bumbled their way through the 169-minute grilling from DCMSC.

An exchange involving Kerry Hopkins, Vice President of Legal and Government affairs at EA, and Damian Collins, Chair of the DCMSC, gained traction online when Collins asked Hopkins whether in-game loot boxes were ethical. Hopkins answered: 'We don't call them loot boxes. What we would [describe them as] is surprise mechanics... People find it fun!'[6]

It is the same 'surprise mechanics' that are regularly used by casinos and bookmakers across the world to momentarily hypnotise players who use their electronic slots and fixed odds betting machines (FOBMs). Published through online outlet *Untamed Science*, Rob Nelson, of the University of Hawaii, analyses the psychology behind slots:

> 'Every time you push down on the "spin" button on a physical slot machine or an online slot, you are taking control in a way that your brain views as positive. Each time you press the button, the visual whirlwind of colours and shapes in front of your eyes release Dopamine in your brain. No matter how many times you push the button, the same thing will happen... This simple yet effective feedback loop boosts feelings of control amongst players which encourages them to ignore the uncertainty of winning or losing and play on for longer.'[7]

It is abundantly clear that there is no difference between the tactics used by EA Sports in their offering of online loot boxes and high street bookmakers virtual slot machines – both are using deceitful tactics to maximise on the revenue from their user base.

In July 2022, the UK government announced that video game loot boxes should not be included in an on-going review of betting law regulation, despite it finding a clear link between the game mechanic and gambling. Rockstar Games' multi-award winning *Grand Theft Auto 5* (*GTAV*) is one of the biggest games created and like EA, isn't immune to its own form of soft gambling, though Rockstar are far less deceitful about the inclusion of gambling as the game, for example, includes a literal online virtual casino for players to use. The purchasing of the game is itself age-restricted to players over eighteen in the UK due to its themes.

GTA is an action-adventure series of games that drops players in a fictional open-world city, where the player is often role-playing as a selection of characters with close links to organised crime. While the game itself is open-world, the player is given an abundance of missions by non-player characters to move the main narrative along; stealing, murders, pimping and car-jacking featuring amongst many other missions, but all with the same purpose – to make as much money as possible.

Due to its violent nature, I was curious as to how easy it would be for someone under 18 years of age to purchase *GTAV* on Microsoft's Xbox Marketplace, buy some in-game currency and gamble it in the virtual in-game casino; all whilst using fake details. I set up the fake profile, with a fake name and birthday (with no age or user verification checks), added my personal debit card onto said account (which of course was registered in an entirely different name to the one on the profile) and purchased the *GTAV* game within 90 seconds of creating the fake profile. Within five minutes of the game installing, I had purchased £10 worth of in-game currency.

I was sad – not shocked – to see how easy it was to set up a fake account and make a micro-transaction that quickly. Within twenty minutes I was sitting at a virtual roulette table, with other virtual characters controlled remotely by real players, ready to gamble the virtual currency in which I had just paid real money for, not even half an hour earlier. It is obvious how relatively easy, and dangerous, it is for players to invest real currency in a virtual economy with no legitimate option to 'cash out' from the game. It is for this reason that the online Casino in *GTAV* is blocked in over 50 countries with strict gambling laws; countries including Greece, Portugal and the UAE.[8]

There is an increasing problem with the messy world of online gambling, whether it be loot boxes or virtual casinos. A problem that is readily accessible 24 hours a day, you can play relatively undetected from the comfort of your own home, whilst unconsciously obtaining a decreased perception of the value of the real cash being electronically gambled.

Rebecca Cassidy, a Goldsmiths Professor and anthropologist of gambling, explored such impulses in her monumental book *Vicious Games* which depicts various gambling experiences. One particularly memorable example being with an anonymous working class man in a high street bookies:

> 'You can't tell a bloke that he can't have a bet! It's the right of every Englishman to have a bet! What next? Ascot won't be royal? The Grand National will be steeplechase number 59! Do me a favour! You may as well have surrendered to the Germans all them years ago to tell a man he can't have a bet!'[9]

It could be argued that one reason the UK government is not doing as much as they could be is because it could impose on what the anonymous man frames as a patriotic right to 'have a bet'.

In 2014, a 15 percent tax on all profits generated from regulated betting was introduced. As video game gambling is not legally gambling, there is no tax income generated from this part of the game. This tax works, partly, in the punters' favour because they no longer have to pay tax on any of their withdrawn winnings. This tax also ensures that the UK economy benefits greatly from the continued growth of the industry, so it is fair to suggest that keeping the gambling industry thriving is in the interest of those in power – another reason why more legislative action may be frowned upon.

Until priorities change, loot boxes and similar forms of soft gambling are likely to remain rife in video games.

Have you ever bet on the Grand National? Write YES or NO in the space below. *If you're unable, I just want you to think about your answer for a moment.*

Chapter 2

Disaster + Capitalism = Risk

What was the last show or film you were recommended to watch on a streaming service and did it meet your hopes? Write your answer in the space below. *If you're unable, I just want you to think about your answer for a moment.*

There is no denying that 2020 onwards has been a disaster for theatres, artists and audiences worldwide, with revenue streams having 'vanished overnight with the shutdown of theatres'[1] due to the COVID-19 pandemic. Whilst the pandemic has birthed moments of collaboration within artistic communities, the knighted billionaires of Theatreland continue to dominate a decimated landscape and, as cultural gatekeepers, refuse to offer any viable solutions to the problems they help enable; all whilst showing a clear lack of empathy and understanding for smaller organisations, companies and creatives.

The proximity of art, capitalism, risk (in relation to programmes of work, how they are marketed, consumed and by whom), and the predatory nature of industry leaders is extremely worrying and growingly pertinent. The COVID-19 outbreak has become an exciting opportunity for big-business and therefore, an increased chance for big profit. This is the first sign of disaster capitalism. Academic Jørgen Randers argues:

> 'Capitalism is carefully designed to allocate capital to the most profitable projects…It is profitable to let the world go to hell. I believe that the tyranny of the short-term will prevail over the decades to come. As a result, a number of long-term problems will not be solved, even if they could have been, and even as they cause gradually increasing difficulties.'[2]

During the pandemic, headlines were aplenty with rumours of nepotism and cronyism in the awarding of contracts to companies to aid the recovery from the pandemic. Campaign group Transparency International UK identified 73 contracts worth more than £3.7 billion in total[3] that required further examination into corruption. 65 of these contracts, to a total of £2.9 billion, were for the procurement, creation and delivery of Personal Protection Equipment. They go on to state that 'between February and November 2020, 98.9 percent of COVID-19 related contracts by value (£17.8 billion) were awarded without any form of competition, many without adequate justification.'[4]

When we look at the initial fallout of the pandemic, the level of handling from the Conservative government and some industry leaders can only be described as, in my opinion, a disaster. Journalist Naomi Klein birthed the term 'Disaster Capitalism'[5] in *The Shock Doctrine: The Rise of Capitalism Disaster,* in which she observes that privatisation, government deregulation, and deep cuts to social spending are often imposed after a mega disaster. Whilst Klein's term is often-used for environmental disasters, the exploitation tactics used within can be seen embedded in the theatre industry's response to the COVID-19 pandemic. A trait pertinent to disaster capitalism and theatre is wealth inequality – the rich with resources to navigate disaster and the 'poor' left to fend for themselves, wondering where their next bit of income will come from. Writer Hein Marais reminds us to: 'shelve the abiding fiction that disasters do not discriminate – that they flatten everything in their path with democratic disregard. Plagues zero in on the disposed, on those forced to build their lives in danger'.[6]

The 'danger' that Marais describes can be compared to the precarity of freelancers struggling to find their next source of income. Where the wealthy are less likely to sit in a state of pandemic-precariousness, the 'disposed' (i.e. freelance artists) will struggle without significant subsidiaries from the government or tools of support. In *Towards A Civic Theatre,* Dan Hutton highlights how socio-politics and exploitative cultural gatekeepers are intrinsically entwined:

> 'In some ways, British theatre has the same problem as the Conservative Party. Both are institutions which relentlessly court the loudest, wealthiest, whitest people. They give this group exactly what they want, exactly when they want it, responding and backtracking when they get irate about something. They pursue these people readily and vehemently, getting better and better at figuring out their needs and desires whilst at the same time finding more creative ways to squeeze money out of them to make the books balance. For the time being, it's working a treat.'[7]

Hutton's point eerily echoes the way in which gambling companies operate, with exploitative methods designed to drain players of their hard-earned cash.

Relentlessly playing *FIFA Ultimate Team* with my friends and watching live Premier League football were absolute staples of my working class upbringing. As I dive further into the messy world of soft gambling, I keep questioning whether, as an artist, I can define my theatre-going as a different kind of soft gambling, one inherently far less dangerous than the *Grand Theft Auto V* online casino or *FIFA Ultimate Team* loot boxes – but one that still carries the prospect of risk.

We first have to acknowledge that working class artists and audiences still face barriers in engaging with certain cultural venues and organisations in the arts industry. When only one in 10 theatre directors are from a working class background[8] there is no surprise that the working class may not feel as though theatre is a place for them, a place where work isn't created, produced, nor programmed with them in mind.

Where one would most likely associate a team like Manchester City FC with an attractive and exciting style of play, consumers and makers of live art may associate specific theatre buildings, companies, artistic directors, with a certain level of artistic quality, thus reducing the risk in them booking a ticket to one of their shows. Much like a football manager trying to implement a certain style of play in their team, theatres and companies try to implement a blueprint into their programme of work – both are leaders wanting to draw new spectators to their philosophies and attract the world's best talent to collaborate and therefore retain more audiences/fans.

But if gatekeepers of the arts, specifically artistic directors and lead programmers, are not diverse themselves then how can anyone expect their audience outreach to be successful enough to draw in people who may have never interacted with live art before? Historically, theatre has been run by very similar people who look very similar and grew up in very similar socio-economic surroundings.

> 'There used to be a template for the artistic directors of theatres. A template about as restricted as candidates for the Tory party leadership. White and male. Obviously. This was so continuous with the default position for power in Britain that for ages it went unremarked. Not any more.'[9]

Although critic Susannah Clapp makes a fantastic observation here, her article fails to acknowledge the prospect of working class leaders in this argument and how 'class is often absent from discussions about diversity in theatre'.[10] We still have a way to go in getting working class artists in buildings where they were, and ultimately still are, unwelcome. As journalist Chantelle Fiddy is quoted during an interview in *Inner City Pressure*:

> 'There's a core issue with many... they simply can't see past their own socio-economic background and class reference points. Pitching Wiley features to *Mixmag* in 2003, they'd say "no-one has heard of him". Which is true, if you asked the attendees at Cream and Ministry of Sound, but if you walked through Mile End with him, he was a street demi-god. It's narrow mindedness, and it perpetuates social division and the underachievement of any act not appealing to [the] middle class.'[11]

Thankfully, things have started to change at the top of organisations. Programmes of works are telling a broader range of stories. Programmes such as New Diorama Theatre's ground-breaking Intervention 01 – a radical stopping of public performances to give artists 'space, time and resource to fund artistic dreamtime, messy new ideas and genuine R&D for companies taking part – with no pressure for programming or any immediate outcomes.'[12] Artistic Director David Byrne explains of the project:

> 'Post-pandemic, we promised to listen more and do better. The sheer catalytic energy required to "bring theatre back" has left artists on the brink of burn-

out and exhaustion. So New Diorama are going to do the most radical thing we can imagine: stop. Marking a once-in-a-generation moment, we'll work behind the scenes to return in 2023 with a renewed artistic vision, a re-energised artist family, and our boldest-ever slate of work.'[13]

There is still a long way to go in terms of class representation. Because of the history and coveted reputation some theatres have, there can still be barriers to access for both diverse audiences and artists engaging with the arts. In 1979, academic John McGrath insisted during a talk at Cambridge University:

> 'there is a working class audience for theatre in Britain which makes demands, and which has values, which are different from those enshrined in our idealised middle class audience'[14]

McGrath's point, made over forty years ago, remains. The conundrum of how to entice working class audiences into auditoriums isn't going to be solved until the work programmed (and therefore the artists employed) are representative enough for an audience to engage with. During her position as artistic director of the Octagon theatre in Bolton, Elizabeth Newman observed theatres need to be 'risk-aware, not risk-averse. The greatest risk we can take is not to take any risks'.[15] If a theatre is not willing to take a risk, how can they expect audiences to do the same themselves?

You only have to look at the way in which theatres such as London's Royal Court and the Soho Theatre are marketed or received, and the way in which they are branded as 'the writers' theatre'[16] and a 'vibrant producer of new theatre, comedy and cabaret'[17] respectively. The proposition for audiences is clear: if you want to see a play written by an exciting 'writer' then go to the Royal Court. If you want to see a 'vibrant' piece of new theatre, go to the Soho Theatre. If you are to go by those self-marketed descriptions of those specific theatres, going anywhere else to see a vibrant piece of new theatre could be seen as a risk.

How could theatres manage this variation of audience risk? How could they enable audiences to take a gamble on entering a space that has for a long time been systematically against non-white middle class people?

The self-marketed descriptions of those specific theatres are created in a way in which assures a minimisation of risk for audiences; a season ticket option would absorb that risk. These theatres can be seen as heterotopias of ritual, isolated and not freely accessible. The ritual embedded here being the transaction of handing over substantial sums of money.

A variation of a season ticket type structure would be rewarding consumers for their loyalty to a theatre. For example, for every two production tickets purchased, they would receive a free ticket to a more radical piece of work. In 2018, a YouGov poll was released to analyse how the British public felt about loyalty schemes and how they benefited brands with the report revealing that:

> 'People are willing to put their money where their loyalty cards are. Among consumers using loyalty programmes, almost half (47%) spend more with a brand whose scheme they are a member of, whilst four in ten (38%) are more likely to recommend the brand. What's more, more than a quarter (28%) say they feel "emotionally connected" with a brand whose programme they belong to.'[18]

The logistics of creating a loyalty scheme across large-scale commercial venues would be difficult to cohesively deploy and subsequently manage but ticketing memberships are already in place, they are just not affordable to working class people.

Whilst the National Theatre and the Royal Court offer membership schemes ranging from £25 to £12,000[19], they do not include free tickets. Sure, if you had £12,000 spare to donate to a theatre then you are more likely to be able to absorb the cost of a pair of tickets but placing the choice of which show to purchase tickets for on an audience member, rather than from the theatre, minimises the chance of said audience member taking a risk on viewing a production that is unusual to what they would usually view.

There are, however, a host of ticketing schemes already aimed at increasing affordability, which enables audiences to minimise their risk in viewing a production. These schemes are often subsidised by corporations with the primary aim of acting as a vehicle for their branding, whilst also, in some cases, acting as tax write-offs.

Foreign currency exchange company Travelex have subsidised hundreds of tickets per show at the National Theatre since their sponsorship started in 2003, the theatre uniquely placed to deliver a high-brand recognition for Travelex. Corporate sponsorship and subsidiaries are rife. The Old Vic partners with corporate finance accounting services PwC[20] whilst the Barbican with AV solutions company Christie Digital[21] and the list goes on.

Every theatre will have a list on their website of substantial donors that partner with certain productions or seasons. Without substantial government subsidies, the leaders of these theatres are continually forced to get creative in order to ensure longevity in their (and their board members') goals and ambitions.

A successful high-profile case of 'pin-wielding critics' rallying against corporate sponsorship saw the Royal Shakespeare Company (RSC) dropping their subsidised ticket sponsor BP in 2019 due to a nationwide group of school students signing a petition threatening to boycott RSC productions because of its links to the fossil fuel company. There is no denying that by corporations such as BP and Travelex subsidising and sponsoring ticket schemes, there is a greater opportunity for an increase in audience engagement, leading to a needed boost in ticket sales but much like in the case of BP, it raises ethical dilemmas on how much of our souls we are willing to sell to scale up affordability and longevity in survival of art to dilute risk.

Theatre criticism, write-ups and reviews continue to be crucial for ticket-buyers and show producers alike. In such an industry driven by PR and marketing, a prominent critic reviewing a show is, in some way, comparable to receiving a tip-off from an industry insider in the football. You'd feel much more comfortable placing a bet on the transfer of a player to another club having received some tips from a trusted source who knew what they were talking about. This is just another tool capable of aiding in the spectators' risk assessment on a production – if a trusted critic reviews a show unfavourably it would suggest that the show would not be worth the risk and vice versa with positive reviews.

After consciously (or subconsciously) analysing all the supporting materials laid out, the prospective spectator would then be in an informed position to make a decision on whether the 'stake' of buying a ticket would give a worthy return on their investment of time and money – or not worth the gamble at all.

A list of every reason why someone might gamble would be endless. Much like going to the theatre for a dose of escapism, the thrill of the chase or the prospect of riches through traditional forms of gambling such as casinos and online betting, the act itself is seen as an immersive event. Philip Mawer's *Overcoming Gambling* highlights such an event first hand:

> 'When I was gambling, be it in a bookmakers', at a race track, in a casino or logged on to an internet gaming site, I entered a "twilight zone" in my mind. It was rather like a trance in that the real world was blocked out, and all my stresses and pressures, problems and issues were put to one side. I focused on the form page, the running of a race, the spin of a wheel, turn of a card or roll of a dice, and nothing else mattered.'[22]

Alongside going to the theatre whenever I can afford it, one relatively low-cost activity I also do in order to access the 'twilight zone' mentioned is to sit down in front of the TV after a long day, inevitably scroll endlessly through Netflix's offerings, eventually watch a film or TV show. With 222 million worldwide subscribers[23], Netflix has undoubtedly changed the way in which we interact with art in the digital age. For one fixed monthly fee of £10.99, you can stream over 4,220+ movies and more than 1,980 TV shows from a wide variety of genres on your device at any time. Due to the sheer volume and variety of content available, £10.99 per month must then be considered a low-risk gamble. That's without considering other streaming platforms also available, with more appearing on a semi-regular basis.

It is this twilight zone where I recognise the biggest similarity between soft gambling and art. These are the reasons I continue to take a risk on a theatre ticket; to escape. Does that make me a theatre addict? Am I addicted to going to the theatre? In that sense, I acknowledge then that I am lucky that this particular addiction is not one that can cause me (or those around me) harm. But it does make me realise my affinity to more serious interactions.

What do you do to escape? Interpret 'escape' as you wish and write your answer in the space below. *If you're unable, I just want you to think about your answer for a moment.*

Chapter 3:
Football Flutter

Have you ever made a cash bet with a friend, over something daft, for fun? What was the bet? Write your answer in the space below. *If you're unable, I just want you to think about your answer for a moment.*

We've looked at various forms of 'soft gambling' that can often slip into the periphery, from video games to a night out at the theatre, but it would be foolish to not mention a very prominent form of gambling that has devastating reach: football.

There is no denying that the sport of football (or 'soccer') is viewed as 'a central aspect of contemporary British, European and even global culture.'[1] Over the past twenty years the sport has seen a substantial increase in investment, revenue and can be acknowledged for birthing some of the planet's biggest and richest celebrities. With some of the world's greatest players, such as Lionel Messi, earning $130 million in 2022[2], it is easy to see the appeal of the glamorous high-roller life on offer and why sports stars, like Messi, are idolised by sports fans everywhere.

Football has endured a long and complicated relationship with the betting industry. Even though gambling is 'emblazoned across the chests of idolised sports stars'[3], professional players, managers and club members are 'prohibited from betting, either directly or indirectly, on any football match or competition that takes place anywhere in the world.'[4] This has not stopped betting companies exploiting the audiences of the money-laden sport, in which the majority of its consumers are more likely to be from lower socio-economic backgrounds. It raises the question why, unlike France where in 1991 tobacco and alcohol sponsorships were banned across the sport, that there has not been stronger restrictions imposed in the UK to protect those at risk of developing an unhealthy relationship with gambling?

Because of the recent rise in pay-to-watch televised games, stadium sponsorships have also sky-rocketed. This can be in the form of obtaining stadium naming rights (Stoke City's Bet365 Stadium as one example) or hiring small billboards that surround the pitch itself for a season, which are extremely prominent during televised or recorded broadcasts. Research by Goldsmiths University in 2017 found 'gambling logos or branding were on screen for between 71 percent and 89 percent of *Match of the Day* programmes'[5] even though the BBC does not carry any direct advertising. It is this level of exposure that is changing the relationship between the working class spectator and the betting companies.

Dr Darragh McGee, lecturer for the University of Bath, believes that betting is having a detrimental impact on the way in which younger viewers interact with the sport:

> 'A new generation of sports fans view gambling as vital to their enjoyment of sport [and that] an accelerated sports culture in which the casual staking of money is an essential accompaniment to watching the game.'[6]

As a working class spectator who has bet on football many times – both in-person at the high street bookies and online – I know first-hand the point Dr McGee makes. I have felt before that a bet can make an otherwise dull game much more interesting, irrespective of whether one even supports either of the two teams playing. If younger viewers are desensitised to the health and financial risks involved in gambling, it can spark an interest at an early age that has the potential to develop into something sinister.

As it is often believed, 'football is a sport riddled with randomness'[7] and nobody could have expected Leicester City Football Club to be crowned champions of the English Premier League at the end of the 2015/2016 season. Leicester City FC were bottom of the 20-team league just 12 months prior so their rise to the top could simply not have been foreseen. Leading UK betting companies were so confident that this wouldn't happen that they offered odds of a staggering 5,000/1, meaning a £1 stake would have returned an eye-watering sum of £5001. Bookmakers across the country immediately regretted the offering of these generous odds having lost 'over £25m as lucky punters bagged upwards of £100,000'.[8] The Leicester pay-outs break the record for the biggest loss in British sporting history.

The betting industry utilising and ultimately monetising popular culture is not a new phenomenon, but it is one we must look at with caution. Bookmakers up and down the country have long offered more and more ridiculous scenarios to bet on. Paddy Power have forged a reputation as an industry-leading organisation for, even after the Leicester City FC upset, offering high odds on ludicrous events as a ploy to boost marketing. You could bet on Elvis Presley being found alive and well at 1000/1, Kim Kardashian to be the US President in the next 10 years at 2000/1 and the Pope to play for Rangers FC at 4000/1.

Former Paddy Power Managing Director Christian Woolfelden has described their marketing tactics as mischievously disruptive by stating that:

> "Central to our innovative marketing strategy is the need to keep creating unique, engaging and highly disruptive brand activities. That's where mischief comes in. Locked in a dark room, with no day-to-day responsibilities, their only mission in life is to come up with ingenious ways of entertaining our potential audience and they are a force to be reckoned with."[9]

According to a recent study by Statista, the UK sportsbook sector favours Paddy Power as the leading website by share of voice, accounting for 5.9 percent during the second quarter 2022[10]. Following this, the

Telegraph and William Hill ranked in second and third place respectively. This focus on strong and disruptive digital marketing is clearly working.

In 2019, the Gambling Commission released findings from research undertaken about the UK population's views on gambling corporations advertising with the report 'exploring how gambling advertising influences opinions, motivations and gambling behaviours'[11]. This report presented some interesting observations.

1. Despite attitudes to gambling being mostly positive and permissive – attitudes towards gambling advertising overall were predominantly negative. The primary issue cited for holding negative perceptions was the sheer volume of advertising.
2. Respondents felt that 'more serious' types of gambling should be bound by tighter advertising rules. Online gambling types were felt to require tighter advertising regulation, due to ease of access and a perceived lack of barriers to risky play.
3. The prevalence of gambling advertising in sport was a complex issue – most felt the volume was excessive, but some felt gambling had a positive impact on sport.
4. Most felt more regulation was needed to limit the amount of gambling advertising young people are exposed to when engaging with sport.

5. While there has been a shift in responsible industry advertising, with respondents feeling that they have seen more about safer gambling in recent years, they still believe there is scope for improvement.

The report provokes an uneasy unspoken consensus; that gambling is fine in moderation. That gambling safeguarding campaigns are rising in profile. That 'risky play' should be regulated tighter. The Gambling Commission defines a gambling opportunity as risky play where:

> 'the speed and frequency of the gambling opportunity within a game impacts the risk. Activities that permit high frequency participation are more likely to be associated with harm and more readily facilitate problematic behaviour, such as loss chasing. … Higher risk products typically provide players with the opportunity for fast-paced, repetitive and chance-based games which are available 24 hours a day. … Activities with high event frequency are likely to be the most attractive.'[12]

According to a study done by Classic Football Shirts, in the 2022/23 Premier League season, eight out of the 20 teams (40 percent) feature a gambling sponsor on their shirt[13] compared with the 1992/93 season where there was a much more even spread of sponsor industries, with electrical companies and organisations accounting for 23 percent that year. Due to the rise of betting sponsors in various forms, there have been a variety of charities and organisations set up to campaign for an end to their involvement. The Big Step is one example, who campaign to end all gambling advertising and sponsorship in football. In their own words, 'we are a campaign to end all gambling advertising and sponsorship in football, led by people harmed by gambling. We are part of Gambling with Lives, a community of families bereaved by gambling-related suicide.'[14]

In July 2022, they published an open letter to all Premier League Clubs, signed by over 100 people with a relationship to gambling. The letter expressed disappointment that the Government's Gambling Act review white paper was postponed by the Conservative Party Leadership contest following Boris Johnson's resignation as Prime Minister. Much like the aforementioned DCMSC report on loot boxes, it is expected that there will be an abundance of proposals here, but not much concrete legislative change to protect vulnerable people. The Big Steps' letter is worth reading and considering in full:

> We are writing to you as a group of over 100 people harmed by gambling to urge you to vote to end gambling sponsorship.

We are people who have been addicted to gambling, who have been negatively affected by someone else's gambling or who have lost loved ones to gambling-related suicide. Public Health England estimates that there are 409 deaths related to gambling every year in England alone, while a YouGov study from this year shows that 2.9 million people are either already addicted or at risk of being so, with a further 3.3 million classified as "affected others". These stark figures show what we already know: gambling harm is not an issue affecting just a small minority, it is severely harming – sometimes killing – many in your community.

Together, we have spent three years campaigning to end gambling sponsorship in football and our priority and focus is government legislation to do so. Relying on clubs to self-regulate has not worked so far, the consequence being 700 gambling adverts in one Premier League match and the same brands appearing in kids sections on club websites, in matchday programmes, and in sticker books.

We are saddened that the Gambling Act review white paper has been delayed yet again, but the government are delaying the inevitable. We are in no doubt that one government, one day will do what multiple European countries such as Spain, Italy, Belgium and the Netherlands have already done and restrict the obscene levels of gambling marketing in Football.

Despite our preference for government action, we still believe football can do the right thing regardless of what policy-makers do and when they do it. We will continue to campaign to parliament throughout this legislative process, but we are also urging you to vote to end gambling sponsorship. It is the very least your clubs can do to prevent the devastation we experienced happening to anyone else.

Rest assured we will be encouraging clubs at all levels and in all countries to do the same – this is not exclusively an issue for Premier League fans.

The stakes are high. The mass promotion of addictive products through our national sport is not normal or safe. Football – at all levels – is worshipped and trusted by millions of young fans around the world and that is why the game should not be hijacked to push online casinos, especially on shirts.

You are not just corporate entities, you are influential and trusted hubs of your community. That is why you must take responsibility to safeguard all your fans – especially children – from something which takes hundreds of lives every year.

A vote to end gambling sponsorship must be the start of comprehensive action that extends beyond the front of your shirts. Doing it alone is incoherent. If you vote to accept the principle that gambling ads on shirts are harmful, then the same must apply to the same logos on sleeves, for the adverts that flash around your pitch, in your stadium and on your club's website.

In doing so, you would be doing something that would be extremely popular amongst your supporters. There is overwhelming desire and evidence to end all gambling advertising in football, with nearly 100,000 fans signing petitions and dozens of UK and Irish clubs now surviving without it and campaigning against it.

We are not anti-gambling and you won't find one prohibitionist amongst us. We are not trying to stop your fans from having a bet on football, nor are we trying to completely end the relationship between gambling and football. Gambling should quite rightly be tolerated and available for adults should they wish, but it should not be promoted, especially in a globally-adored league where young people make up a quarter of the Audience.

We would happily put forward representatives from the below list of signatories to meet with you to discuss this further.

Yours,

Over 100 people harmed by gambling[15]

From Forest Green Rovers to Glasgow City FC, many smaller clubs have signed up to support The Big Steps' call for an eradication of betting sponsors. Whilst there is an ironic risk in clubs pledging support to this scheme solely to aid public relations, there has been a distinct lack of larger clubs – with worldwide reach – supporting it.

Dulwich Hamlet FC, in South West London, are one of the teams who have pledged for the scheme. Having moved to South West London in 2021, I later found myself missing the buzz of attending a live football match. When living in Portsmouth, I would regularly go to Fratton Park to watch the mighty Pompey under the floodlights. The city's morale and the football club's results would go hand in hand – if the club won a game, it felt like the whole city was happy. We lived and breathed football. As travelling back to Portsmouth for the home fixtures was financially stretching, I made the choice, along with a friend, to start going to Dulwich Hamlet FC home games; the Champion Hill stadium a mere 30 minute bus away, tickets only £5 for concessions, and the club seeming morally sound, it was a no brainer. It was a relief to walk into a stadium with no betting sponsors.

At every home game, Dulwich and Hamlet Supporters Trust sell '50/50' tickets. If you're not familiar with the mechanic of a 50/50 half-time draw, think of it as a raffle of sorts, often poised as a fundraising initiative for the club where supporters can win prizes of monetary value, often with a low price per ticket.

There is an interesting complexity in the relationship of charities and not-for-profits and risk. Some organisations, like Dulwich Hamlet Supporters Trust, promote 'risk free' raffles. Gamblers here are positioned to more easily justify their bet, albeit a small stake of fifty pence a go. This can then be proposed as a win-win for the player if their raffle number is called: they get a prize, be it monetary or some 'raffle tat'. If they lose, they've donated to a charity or non-profit and can feel good about that.

There is a similar position with the National Lottery and their operator Camelot.

It could be quite easy for problem gamblers to participate in raffles, the lottery, or buying scratch cards because of the charitable causes that benefit from them playing. The National Lottery players have 'helped to raise over £46 billion for Good Causes, with more than 670,000 individual awards made across the UK – the equivalent of more than 240 lottery grants in every UK postcode district.'[16] With the National Lottery's total ticket sales of £8,090.7 million in the year ending 31st March 2022[17], there are clear arguments for the exceptional good that the National Lottery does in its charitable schemes. There is little doubt that they change lives for the better. But we cannot forget how a problem gambler might exploit this by finding excuses to justify their spending on lottery tickets.

In *Vicious Games*, Dr Rebecca Cassidy points our attention to one person she interviewed at a raffle in Kent:

> 'My heart beats a bit faster when they make the draw and you're looking at your numbers and you might hear it and your heart jumps, but you can't be sure so you read it again and you don't trust your eyes because your heart is just leaping, but you read it a third time and there it is. You've got the winning ticket! Up your hand goes, and people are pleased for you and it might be a lovely plant or a box of chocs, but the lovely thing is you've got a surprise.'[18]

Irrespective of whether participating in a small-scale event in Kent, a jam-packed football stadium in Portsmouth or playing the weekly lottery, the experience of a raffle remains. A stake is placed in order to obtain that adrenaline-fuelled feeling of defying the odds and winning the flutter.

Have you ever bought a ticket in a raffle?
Did you win?
If so, what did you win?
How did you feel?
Write your answer in the space below. *If you're unable, I just want you to think about your answer for a moment.*

Chapter 4:
Cardboard Nostalgia

Can you remember and describe a time you swapped something you like for something you love?
Write your answer in the space below. *If you're unable, I just want you to think about your answer for a moment.*

During the first COVID-19 lockdown, I became addicted to buying packs of *Pokémon* Trading Cards. The *Pokémon* Trading Card Game (TCG) is a collectible card game involving characters in the widely popular *Pokémon* franchise. The first cards were printed in October 1996 by Media Factory in Japan and the game consequentially exploded worldwide, selling a total of 43.2 billion cards worldwide to date.[1]

I have clear and distinct memories of playing the *Pokémon* video game with my friends when I was younger, all of us battling to find the best *Pokémon* we could get our hands on, trading our duplicate cards in order to fill our folders. When we took a rare break from playing the video game, we would walk down to the local shop, place our pocket money on the counter and in return we could get a packet of *Pokémon* cards. In high street stores such as WH Smith, Argos and Sainsburys, you can purchase a booster pack of *Pokémon* TCG for roughly £4.[2] Each booster pack contains ten cards, and much like fine wine or whisky, these packets and cards can vary in price depending on age and rarity. There are various releases each year and the older and rarer the pack, the more money they will fetch on the second-hand market.

One particular sealed box of booster packs, the 1999 *Pokémon* Base Set Shadowless 1st Edition Booster Box, is considered to have sparked English players' and collectors' interest in the hobby. Whilst it is impossible to know how many remain in private hands, many come up for sale on sites such as eBay and specialised Facebook groups. At the time of writing this, there is one factory sealed 1999 Base Set Shadowless 1st Edition Booster Box on sale for £45,000. Numerous articles claim these sets have sold for as much as almost half a million dollars. RRP for the sets were around $100 in 1999.

Similar to loot boxes, certain rare cards offer an in-game boost to the player when played competitively. Whilst the furore continues to rage about the morality of software developers exposing loot boxes to young players, here the official *Pokémon* TCG age rating is 6+.

A recent rise in nostalgic trends making a return to the market (Polaroid cameras being one example) has seen online personalities such as Randolph (who boasts 1.19 million YouTube subscribers[3]), KSI (15.9 million[4]) and Logan Paul (23.6 million[5]) capitalising on this hunger for nostalgia, by venturing into the world of collecting *Pokémon* TCG.

Whether they also have a nostalgic connection to the hobby, or whether they are simply jumping on the Snorlax-sized hype train, *Pokémon* collecting is currently cropping up in every corner of the internet and where there is a frenzy, there is money to be made. Randolph set up online retailer PokeRand, enabling him to push the hobby onto his audiences and make money. PokeRand gives buyers a chance to 'Shop all things *Pokémon*! From the newest Trading Card booster boxes, to vintage single cards to PSA Graded Cards and everything in-between.'[6]

One facet of the hype enabled buyers to purchase single vintage packs from otherwise sealed rare booster boxes. Where buyers may not be able to purchase entire boxes, they could own a piece of history by purchasing a single booster pack and watch Randolph open them on a YouTube livestream. These are dubbed by the hobby community as Box Breaks.[7]

The premise here is clear; you could purchase a rare pack, watch a famous YouTuber (in this case, Randolph) open it up in front of tens of thousands of people, in the hope he pulls out a rare card from your pack, with all your cards then shipped to you the next day. Randolph ran ten separate Box Break shows between 2020 and 2021, with packs available ranging from £12.99 each (*Pokémon* XY Evolutions 2016) to £999 each (Base Set Unlimited 1999).

Whilst marketing campaigns such as Paddy Power's mischievous advertising is overtly in-your-face, strewn across billboards and on television, this kind of risk is a lot more subtle, hiding in TikTok and YouTube virality. Scrolling through these sites you can often see videos of people winning big in casinos or online, via Box Breaks or viral clips of extremely rare cards being pulled into compilations. This kick starts a chain of videos of high-profile YouTubers reacting to others; Randolph reacted to Logan Paul opening two rare vintage Charizard cards in one of his Box Breaks. It's worth noting that Randolph has now stopped running Box Break events, stating that:

> "It went away for the reason I started doing them, why I enjoy doing them, and became, to be honest, it became a scam. It just did. You've got YouTubers out there charging double what these packs are worth."[8]

* * *

We have looked at exploitative practices by people and their organisations across a variety of industries. Whether it be as clear as online sports betting, or a little more cloak-and-dagger like these YouTubers, there are clear similarities to traditional ideas of betting; you stake a certain amount of money in the hope you will gain a profit.

I realised I had a complicated relationship to this hobby after a friend pulled me to one side to ask whether I could afford this new-found nostalgia-induced habit, and it slowly dawned on me that I wasn't chasing the rarity of a card to appreciate the artwork or even to play the game but rather to hunt for the card with the highest net-profit I could find, sell it on eBay and go again. I thought about buying the costly packs from the Box Break events on YouTube, partly to be involved in something that was fashionable but also in the hope that I may win big. I could justify the relentless cardboard conveyor belt of risk to myself as just merely revisiting happy memories of opening booster packs as a kid. If I bought a booster pack that didn't have any high-value cards, I would buy more.

I recognise two points from the NHS questionnaire about problem gambling are pertinent to me here.

- *Have you tried to win back money you have lost (chasing losses)?*
- *Have you borrowed money or sold anything to get money to gamble?*

I can't put a figure on how much I spent on trips to shops like Sainsburys to buy *Pokémon* booster packs, or whether I'm actually in overall profit or not now. But I do know I chased my losses. I do know that I sold other items in my life that I thought I didn't need any more to buy cards. I know I lied about how much I was spending.

Cardboard nostalgia doesn't stop at *Pokémon*. The sports trading card community has boomed over the last few years, according to eBay's State of Trading Cards report, with the number of cards purchased on the site rising 142 percent from 2020 to 2021.[9]

This fad once grew so frenetic that American retailer Target had to 'halt [the] sales of sports cards to protect the safety and security of its employees and customers after a disagreement over the collectibles sparked a fight at a store in Wisconsin.'[10] One store temporarily pausing the sales of cards in stores hasn't slowed down the worldwide market, with brands such as *Match Attax* and *Panini* stickers still widely available in UK corner shops, supermarkets and online. Much like how *Pokémon* was a staple of my childhood, Premier League *Match Attax* were as much of a presence.

I want to take you back to October 2006. Around the time of my ninth birthday.

The first World Cup I can really remember had taken place the summer before. Sven-Göran Eriksson guided us in a, well, less-than-exciting World Cup campaign in Germany. Nine-year-old me was devastated, heart-broken. Not as devastated as my friend Charlie who cried, uncontrollably, when we got kicked out by Portugal in the quarterfinals.

I didn't have school that day because my birthday always falls in the October half term. My friends have always told me that I was lucky because I didn't have to sit in Miss Weeks' science lessons or Mr Kent's tedious PE classes. I could just enjoy the day and celebrate. My mum would always cook me a fry up on the morning of my birthday – exactly how I liked it.

One egg – runny yolk
Two rashers of bacon – well done
One sausage
Two hash browns
Grilled tomatoes
And not forgetting the pièce de résistance... fried bread.

But what are most kids excited for on their birthday?

Presents.

The presents I always got were never big, extravagant, nor that expensive, but I'd like to think I was always grateful for what I got. I wasn't expecting much this year but unbeknownst to me my mum had treated me. Sleepy-eyed, I stumbled downstairs and saw my mum had a mischievous glint in her eye. I look next to her and see one wrapped box and a card. I open the card first because that's what you're meant to do, right? Inside is a crisp £20 note.

I then think, *Well, if that's my main present then what's in the box? A deodorant set? LEGO? A revision book on science to appease Miss Weeks' numerous complaining phone calls to my mum to tell her I was significantly underachieving in her class due to poor concentration that* urgently *needed addressing if I was to ever get anywhere in life?*

Nah.

An entire box of *Match Attax* packs.

These were like gold dust. Cardboard currency in my school. I was instantly rich. Much like with the *Pokémon* Booster Boxes, it was very rare to get your hands on an entire box of *Match Attax* packs, even back in 2006 when a pack of cards cost 35p instead of today's £4. Everybody in my school had the yearly *Match Attax* album, some of which still sell today, if full, for over £200 on eBay.

Much like how the Charizard is the big-win card to get in the *Pokémon* TCG, the 2006/2007 *Match Attax* high-value card was a Cristiano Ronaldo Man of The Match. Everybody on the playground was swapping and trading their cards in the hope of obtaining this special card, with its high skill ratings. The trade of swapping duplicate cards to quickly fill your album engulfed playgrounds. It would be a regular occurrence to find hordes of school children gathering around tables to the repetitive sounds of 'got!', 'need!' and 'swap?' There are specialist sites still operating that facilitate the trading of cards between players for a fixed annual cost. gotneedswap.co.uk charges just £3.95 for their service.

Whilst football trading cards have decreased in popularity, these blind bag mechanics are still made available to purchase by children. The pay-to-win sports start in full football kits, gambling sponsors emblazoned across their chest, and are in the hands of children. While *Match Attax* and *Pokémon* were big parts of my childhood, there weren't really many other options in collectibles, whereas now there are many more franchises exploiting both those hungry for a cardboard nostalgia fix and those discovering trading cards and stickers for the first time; franchises such as F1 Grand Prix (Turbo Attax), *Harry Potter* (Wizarding World), *Minecraft* (Time To Mine), *UFC, Fortnite, Turning Red, Toy Story* and many others that are specifically aimed at adolescent children.

Can you remember and describe a time you swapped something you love for something you hate?
Write your answer in the space below. *If you're unable, I just want you to think about your answer for a moment.*

Conclusion

What was the last thing you regret doing?
Write your answer in the space below. *If you're unable, I just want you to think about your answer for a moment.*

Throughout *No Dice* we have looked at various forms of 'soft gambling' and whether it be trading cards, video games, or Netflix, the act of soft gambling has slipped under the radar for too long. But with betting companies gradually being held accountable for their malpractice, there is a slow shift starting to occur.

In August 2022, Coral, Ladbrokes and Foxy Bingo's parent company Entain Plc were ordered to pay a £17 million fine after failing to enforce player safety and anti-money laundering measures, and has been warned it could lose its UK gambling licence if it happens again.[1] Whilst the £17 million is an unequivocally large sum of money, it only represents an extremely small percentage of Entain's £3.9 billion in annual revenue.[2] The Gambling Commission's investigation looked at activity between 2019 and 2020 and as noted in *Racing Post*, 'predates Entain's launch of its Advanced Responsibility and Care (ARC) initiative last year. Ladbrokes and Coral were fined £5.9m for breaches associated with social responsibility in 2019.'[3]

Their breach of anti-money laundering protocols involved 'a series of customers who deposited large sums online without being subjected to sufficient source of funds reviews, including one customer who deposited £186,000 over a six-month period despite being known to live in social housing.'[4]

The danger of soft gambling is not quickly apparent,

but when you examine deeper and look at past traditional forms of gambling, such as the National Lottery and bookies, there are clear examples of under-regulated activities that are contributing to the ongoing risk epidemic. When you place these forms of gambling next to each other, it makes for a heady cocktail that problem gamblers may find intoxicatingly irresistible.

When you gamble, a new world created in your mind. A world where you win. We've all dreamed of big houses, even if just for a minute. Scrolling through Rightmove for places we know we will most likely never be able to afford. We build these increasingly fictitious worlds in our heads. Worlds of almost infinite possibilities. Worlds where we can fly and worlds where everything bad that's ever happened to you didn't. Worlds of extravagance and lavish living where every opulent whim in the world can be yours with a click of a button. Ferraris. Lamborghinis. Far-flung holidays. A second, third, fourth and fifth home. A fridge fully-stocked, never having to worry about the electric running out or the water being cut off.

A common working class mentality is to be grateful for what you have at all times and put your head down to work hard. Family and community is vitally important and this isn't to say these traits aren't visible across the different socio-economic classes, I'm sure they are, but when a working class gambler gambles, I would propose that they are more likely try and build a world that is most different to theirs. When a person of inordinate wealth gambles fifty pounds, it is a drop in the ocean. When a person from a lower socio-economic background gambles the same fifty pounds, it could be the difference between eating that week or not.

A 2013 report by the Buffalo Research Institute on Addictions showed that 'the poorer the neighbourhood, the higher the risk for problem gambling.'[5] Using a pool of five thousand people between the ages of fourteen to ninety, the study found that problem gambling was twice as likely in neighbourhoods with the highest level of concentrated poverty compared to neighbourhoods with the lowest poverty levels, determined by census factors such as the percentage of people who were unemployed, received public assistance, and/or live in poverty – more than 11 percent were problem gamblers, compared to just 5 percent in neighbourhoods ranking in the top fifth of economic advantage.[6]

'No dice' alludes to an unlucky throw in gambling, 'no go', alluding to lack of progress. We now sit precariously in an age of no dice. As trends and fashions change in modern culture, so will the complexity of gambling and risk. I am writing this exact sentence on the 8th of September 2022, the Gambling Commission White Paper due any day now. As with other books in this Inklings series, the relevance of topics and immediacy means that there is a chance that a monumental shift or change in legislation could happen the day after this is published. I hope that the proposals put forward are not hollow promises for change but have a real lasting impact on preventing problem gamblers. Having first been announced in 2019, the paper is now long overdue and with indication that 'there are 250 to 650 gambling related suicides each year in the UK – 4 percent to 11 percent of total suicides'[7], time is heartbreakingly running out for so many.

At the start of *No Dice*, I showed the NHS questionnaire that helps identify problem gamblers. Whilst originally only using this as source material for context, halfway through writing this book I decided to take the quiz and was surprised to see that I scored 25. To remind you, they defined any score over 8 or higher as potentially being a problem gambler. With stories of addiction often comes reflection and I know, looking back, that I have hurt people and lied to fund a habit of placing bets on sports, buy trading cards, scratch cards and visit online casinos.

Whilst I hope this book can spark a conversation around how risk is integrated in our everyday lives, this book acts as an insight into the brain of a problem gambler – my own brain. My relationship to risk will always be tricky. It's will always be complicated and scary. It is something that I have some more clarity on now, so thank you for joining me on this journey.

Almost every time I have placed a bet I have regretted doing so. I hope you haven't regretted taking a risk on reading this book.

Time for one last game.

Email ONE of the following words to nodicenath@gmail.com and wait for a response. I'll be in touch as soon as possible.

arcaDe
phoenIx
esCobar
evEn

Resources

Gambling Treatment & Support

GamCare / www.gamcare.org.uk
Gordon Moody / www.gordonmoody.org.uk
Red Card Gambling / www.redcardgambling.org

Peer & Family Support

GamAnon / www.gamanon.uk
Gamblers Anonymous / www.gamblersanonymous.org.uk
GamFam / www.gamfam.org.uk
GamLEARN / www.gamlearn.org.uk
The Six To Ten Project / www.thesixtoten.co.uk

Self Exclusion Tools & Resources

GamBan / www.gamban.com
GamStop / gamstop.co.uk
Multi Operator Self-Exclusion Scheme / www.self-exclusion.co.uk

Additional Information

Be Gamble Aware / www.begambleaware.org
The Big Step / the-bigstep.com

Note:
I acknowledge my journey to get to a point where I consider myself a problem gambler has not been conventional. A lot of the process in reaching that point has come through the writing of this book and having conversations with like-minded people, the people who have similar triggers that may usually be dismissed by others as 'not proper gambling'. If the themes of the book resonate, but you feel unable to reach out to the services above you can always drop an email for a chat:
nodicenath@gmail.com

References

Introduction

1. "Definitions of terms." Gambling Commission, 2021. gamblingcommission.gov.uk/about-us/guide/page/definitions-of-terms. Accessed 17 September 2022.
2. "Help for problem gambling." NHS, 8 January 2021. nhs.uk/live-well/addiction-support/gambling-addiction/ nhs.uk/live-well/addiction-support/gambling-addiction/. Accessed 15 August 2022.
3. Ibid.
4. BeGambleAware. begambleaware.org. Accessed 17 September 2022.
5. "People from poor UK areas more likely to be high-risk online gamblers - study." Rob Davies, The Guardian, 12 March 2021. theguardian.com/society/2021/mar/12/people-from-poor-uk-areas-more-likely-to-be-high-risk-online-gamblers-study. Accessed 17 September 2022.
6. Ibid.
7. "Gambling industry fails to meet charity donation target." Rob Davies, The Guardian, 3 May 2019. theguardian.com/society/2019/may/03/gambling-industry-fails-to-meet-target-donation-to-addiction-charity. Accessed 17 September 2022.

8. "Addicted To Gambling... | Russell Brand." Russell Brand, YouTube, 3 April 2019. youtube.com/watch?v=NBM0RBm-jzYc. Accessed 18 August 2022.
9. Scottee, Class. Salamander Street, 2020.
10. "Gambling: Poorer UK towns found to have the most betting shops, study shows." Mary-Ann Russon, BBC News, 23 August 2021. bbc.co.uk/news/business-58300899. Accessed 18 August 2022.

Chapter 1

1. "Lootboxes: Advice to the Gambling Commission from ABSG." Gambling Commission, 13 August 2021. gambling-commission.gov.uk/print/lootboxes-advice-to-the-gambling-commission-from-absg. Accessed 17 September 2022.
2. "Video game market in the United Kingdom - Statistics & Facts." J. Clement, Statista, 10 November 2021. statista.com/topics/1763/gaming-in-the-united-kingdom/. Accessed 17 September 2022.
3. FIFA. ea.com/games/fifa. Accessed 17 September 2022.
4. Ultimate Team. ea.com/games/fifa/ultimate-team. Accessed 17 September 2022.
5. "The Incredible Figures Behind EA Sports' Net Revenue From Ultimate Team." Josh Lawless, Sport Bible, 28 February 2021. sportbible.com/football/news-the-figures-behind-ea-sports-net-revenue-from-ultimate-tea-20210228. Accessed 17 September 2022.
6. "UK Parliament Discussing Predatory Lootbox / Micro-transaction with EA / Epic Games." GrimReaper Alva, YouTube, 20 June 2019. youtube.com/watch?v=jPkyERMb-KU8&t=4496s. Accessed 17 September 2022.
7. "The Psychology of Slot Machines." Rob Nelson, Untamed Science, November 2020. untamedscience.com/blog/the-psychology-of-slot-machines/. Accessed 17 September 2022.

8. "Countries That Have Banned the New GTA Casino and Why." Esports News UK, 26 August 2019. esports-news.co.uk/2019/08/26/countries-that-have-banned-the-new-gta-casino-and-why/. Accessed 17 September 2022.
9. Rebecca Cassidy, Vicious Games: Capitalism and Gambling. Pluto Press, 2020.

Chapter 2

1. "One year on: Theatre leaders on a 'dreadful reckoning' for the industry amid the pandemic." Georgia Snow, 10 March 2021. thestage.co.uk/news/one-year-on-theatre-leaders-on-a-dreadful-reckoning-for-the-industry-amid-the-pandemic. Accessed 17 September 2022.
2. "'It is profitable to let the world go to hell'." Jo Confino, The Guardian, 19 January 2015. theguardian.com/sustainable-business/2015/jan/19/davos-climate-action-democracy-failure-jorgen-randers. Accessed 17 September 2022.
3. "CONCERN OVER CORRUPTION RED FLAGS IN 20% OF UK'S PPE PROCUREMENT." Transparency International UK, 21 April 2021. transparency.org.uk/track-and-trace-uk-PPE-procurement-corruption-risk-VIP-lane. Accessed 17 September 2022.
4. Ibid.
5. Naomi Klein, The Shock Doctrine. Macmillan USA, 2007.
6. "A Plague of Inequality." Hein Marais, Mail & Guardian, 19 May 2006. mg.co.za/article/2006-05-19-a-plague-of-inequality/. Accessed 17 September 2022.
7. Dan Hutton, Towards a Civic Theatre. Bristol: Salamander Street Publishing, 2021.
8. "Just 10% of theatre directors 'are working class' – report." Matthew Hemley, The Stage, 1 January 2019. thestage.co.uk/news/just-10-of-theatre-directors-are-working-class—report. Accessed 17 September 2022.

9. "All change! Meet the new artistic directors shaking up British theatre." Susannah Clapp, The Guardian, 23 June 2019. theguardian.com/stage/2019/jun/23/artistic-directors-shaking-up-british-theatre-lynette-linton-suba-das-tarek-iskander. Accessed 17 September 2022.
10. "'Power has to be grasped': British theatre is battling its class problem." Catherine Love, The Guardian, 13 March 2018. theguardian.com/stage/2018/mar/13/british-theatre-class-problem. Accessed 17 September 2022.
11. Nathalie Olah, Steal As Much As You Can. Watkins Media, 2019.
12. "A season of no shows." New Diorama Theatre, 1 August 2022. newdiorama.com/news/a-season-of-no-shows. Accessed 17 September 2022.
13. Ibid.
14. John McGrath, A Good Night Out. Nick Hern Books, 1996.
15. "The greatest risk in theatre? Not taking any risks." Lyn Gardner, The Guardian, 12 May 2015. theguardian.com/stage/theatreblog/2015/may/12/greatest-risk-in-theatre. Accessed 17 September 2022.
16. royalcourt.com
17. sohotheatre.com
18. "A nation of loyalty members: Three quarters of Brits belong to a loyalty scheme." Amelia Brophy, YouGov, 5 June 2018. yougov.co.uk/topics/politics/articles-reports/2018/06/05/nation-loyalty-members-three-quarters-brits-belong. Accessed 17 September 2022.
19. "Patrons." National Theatre. nationaltheatre.org.uk/support-us/individuals/patrons. Accessed 17 September 2022.
20. "PWC £10 PREVIEWS." The Old Vic. oldvictheatre.com/ticket-info/pwc-10-previews/. Accessed 17 September 2022.
21. "Sponsorship case study: Christie Digital." Barbican. barbican.org.uk/join-support/support-us/for-businesses/sponsorship/case-study-christie-digital. Accessed 17 September 2022.
22. Philip Mawer, Overcoming Gambling. John Murray Press, 2019. p20.

23. "Netflix Revenue and Usage Statistics (2022)." Mansoor Iqbal, Business of Apps, 3 August 2022. businessofapps.com/data/netflix-statistics/. Accessed 17 September 2022.

Chapter 3

1. Anne Eyre, Football and religious experience: sociological reflections. Religious Experience Research Centre, 1997.
2. "Lionel Messi." Forbes. forbes.com/profile/lionel-messi/. Accessed 17 September 2022.
3. Rebecca Cassidy, Vicious Games: Capitalism and Gambling. Pluto Press, 2020.
4. "KNOW THE RULES: BETTING, MATCH FIXING AND INSIDE INFORMATION." The FA. thefa.com/football-rules-governance/policies/betting-rules. Accessed 17 September 2022.
5. "Frequency, duration and medium of advertisements for gambling and other risky products in commercial and public service broadcasts of English Premier League football." Rebecca Cassidy, Niko Ovenden, Research Online, 2017. research.gold.ac.uk/id/eprint/20926/. Accessed 17 September 2022.
6. "Revealed: the 'dire consequences' of football's relationship with gambling." David Conn, The Guardian, 10 January 2019. theguardian.com/football/2019/jan/10/football-gambling-dire-consequences-young-men-bet-new-study. Accessed 17 September 2022.
7. James Tippett, The Football Code: The Science of Predicting the Beautiful Game. 2017.
8. "Leicester win Premier League title: Bookmakers' set to lose over £25m as lucky punters bag £100,000 winnings." Jack de Menezes, Independent, 3 May 2016. independent.co.uk/sport/football/premier-league/leicester-win-the-premier-league-odds-bookmakers-to-lose-over-ps25m-lucky-punters-bag-ps100-000-payout-a7010726.html. Accessed 17 September 2022.

9. "How Paddy Power's mischievous marketing strategy paid off." Christian Woolfenden, Hot Topics. hottopics.ht/15499/how-paddy-powers-innovative-marketing-strategy-paid-off/. Accessed 17 September 2022.
10. "Leading sportsbook-related websites in the United Kingdom (UK) in 2nd quarter 2022, by share of voice." Daniela Coppola, Statista, 9 August 2022. statista.com/statistics/960732/leading-sportsbook-websites-by-sov-united-kingdom-uk/. Accessed 17 September 2022.
11. "Statistics and research." Gambling Commission. gamblingcommission.gov.uk/statistics-and-research/publication/consumer-attitudes-towards-gambling-advertising-2019-research. Accessed 17 September 2022.
12. "Guidance to licensing authorities." Gambling Commission. gamblingcommission.gov.uk/manual/guidance-to-licensing-authorities/the-gambling-product-what-are-the-issues-higher-risk-products. Accessed 17 September 2022.
13. "Premier League Sponsors 2022/23
14. Once again the Premier League is dominated by gambling sponsors with 8/20 teams featuring a gambling sponsor on their shirts for this season.
15. Compare that to the inaugural Premier League season where there was a much wider spread in sponsors." @classicshirts, Twitter. 8 August 2022, 6:00pm, twitter.com/classicshirts/status/1556686829843369986/photo/2. Accessed 17 September 2022.
16. About The Big Step. the-bigstep.com/about.
17. "Over 100 people write to PL clubs ahead of crucial gambling vote." The Big Step, 25 July 2022. the-bigstep.com/home/f/over-100-people-write-to-pl-clubs-ahead-of-crucial-gambling-vote. Accessed 17 September 2022.
18. "Where the money goes." National Lottery. national-lottery.co.uk/life-changing/where-the-money-goes. Accessed 17 September 2022.
19. Ibid.
20. Rebecca Cassidy, Vicious Games. Pluto Press, 2020.

Chapter 4

1. "*Pokémon* Trading Card Game." Wikipedia. en.wikipedia.org/wiki/*Pokémon*_Trading_Card_Game. Accessed 17 September 2022.
2. "Pokemon Sleeved Booster." Sainsbury's. sainsburys.co.uk/gol-ui/product/all-summer/pokemon-sleeved-booster. Accessed 17 September 2022.
3. "Randolph." YouTube. youtube.com/c/OfficialRandolph. Accessed 17 September 2022.
4. "JJ Olatunji." YouTube. youtube.com/user/KSIOlajidebtHD. Accessed 17 September 2022.
5. "Logan Paul." YouTube. youtube.com/c/loganpaulvlogs. Accessed 17 September 2022.
6. pokerand.net
7. "Box Breaks." pokerand.net/collections/box-breaks
8. "Why I QUIT *Pokémon* Box Breaks." Randolph Pokemon, YouTube, 10 February 2021. youtube.com/watch?v=f6Xx-RAdXR20. Accessed 17 September 2022.
9. "eBay's 2021 "State of Trading Cards" Report Spotlights Collecting Trends and Industry Predictions." eBay News Team, eBay, 11 February 2021. ebayinc.com/stories/news/ebays-2021-state-of-trading-cards-report-spotlights-collecting-trends-and-industry-predictions/. Accessed 17 September 2022.
10. "Target halts sale of trading cards, including *Pokémon*, over safety concerns." Minyvonne Burke, NBC News, 14 May 2021. nbcnews.com/news/us-news/target-halts-sale-trading-cards-including-pok-mon-over-safety-n1267442. Accessed 17 September 2022.

Conclusion

1. "Ladbrokes Owner Hit With Record Fine and Warned License At Risk." Thomas Seal, Bloomberg, 17 August 2022. bloomberg.com/news/articles/2022-08-17/ladbrokes-owner-hit-with-record-fine-and-warned-license-at-risk. Accessed 17 August 2022.
2. Ibid.
3. "Ladbrokes Coral owner Entain fined record £17 million over regulatory failures." Scott Burton, Racing Post, 17 August 2022. racingpost.com/news/ladbrokes-coral-owner-entain-fined-record-17-million-over-regulatory-failures/573818. Accessed 17 September 2022.
4. Ibid.
5. "People in poor neighborhoods are twice as likely to have gambling problems, study finds." Cathy Wilde, University at Buffalo, 3 January 2014. buffalo.edu/news/releases/2014/01/001.html. Accessed 17 September 2022.
6. Ibid.
7. "Gambling with Lives." UK Parliament. committees.parliament.uk/writtenevidence/2093/pdf/. Accessed 17 September 2022.

About the Author

Nathan Charles is a working class producer, theatre-maker and director from Portsmouth. He completed his MA in Theatre & Performance at The University of Chichester in 2021 after completing a three-year BA in Acting. He is also Co-Artistic Director of Brightmouth Productions, Co-Editor of *The Crumb* and Co-Founder of devised comedy group Red Biscuit Theatre. Nathan's work focuses on challenging our existing relationships with socio-economic issues, with a particular focus on class and gambling. Also, when he's clean shaven he looks like Russell from the 2009 Pixar film *Up*.

About the Inklings series

This book is part of 404 Ink's Inkling series which presents big ideas in pocket-sized books.

They are all available at 404ink.com/shop.

If you enjoyed this book, you may also enjoy these titles in the series:

The New University: Local Solutions to a Global Crisis – James Coe

The New University considers the enormous challenge of reimagining how our public realm can function in a post-COVID landscape, and the institutions that form an indelible part of our civic life. Coe reimagines the University as a more civic and personal institution, believing we can get there through realigning our research to communal benefit.

Blind Spot: Exploring and Educating on Blindness – Maud Rowell

When it comes to blindness, people can often have many questions and few answers. In *Blind Spot*, Maud educates about the realities of living with sight loss, offering the knowledge they need to become better, more tolerant members of diverse communities.

Now Go: On Grief and Studio Ghibli – Karl Thomas Smith

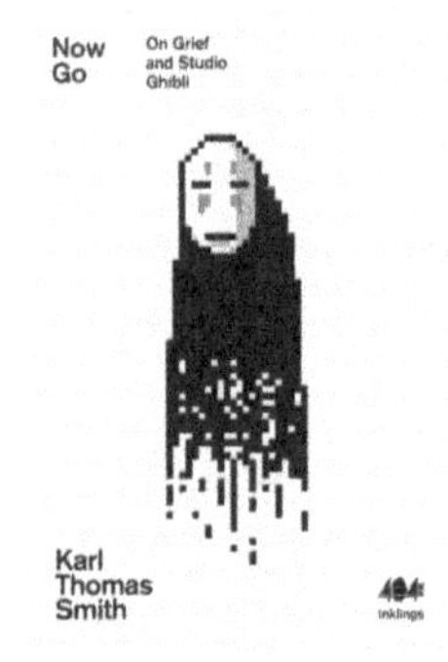

Grief is all around us. At the heart of the brightly coloured, vividly characterised, joyful films of Studio Ghibli, they are wracked with loss – of innocence, of love, of the connection to our world and of that world itself. *Now Go* enters these emotional waters to interrogate not only how Studio Ghibli navigates grief so well, but how that informs our own understanding of grief's manifold faces.